The Rise and Fall of Little Voice

A Drama in Two Acts

by Jim Cartwright

A SAMUEL FRENCH ACTING EDITION

SAMUEL FRENCH

FOUNDED 1830

SAMUELFRENCH.COM

ISBN   978-0-573-69565-0   Printed   in   U.S.A.   #19972

MUSIC USE NOTE

IMPORTANT BILLING AND CREDIT REQUIREMENTS

The play opened at Cottesloe Theatre, Royal National Theatre, London on 16th June 1992:

MARI HOFF	Alison Steadman
LV	Jane Horrocks
PHONE MAN	George Raistrick
BILLY	Adrian Hood
SADIE	Annette Badland
RAY SAY	Pete Postlethwaite
MR BOO	George Raistick
MUSICIANS:	
(keyboards)	Terry Davies
(drums)	Michael Gregory
Director	Sam Mendes
Designer	William Dudley

This production subsequently transferred to the Aldwych Theatre, West End, London on October 1992 with the same cast.

It received its regional premiere in August 1993 at Theatre Royal, Bristol.

The American premiere opened at Steppenwolf Theatre, Chicago, on 12th December 1993:

```
MARI HOFF----------------------------Rondi Reed
LV ----------------------------------Hynden Walch
PHONE MAN --------------------------Alan Wilder
BILLY ------------------------------- Ian Barford
SADIE ------------------------------- Karen Vaccaro
RAY SAY ----------------------------George Innes
MR BOO------------------------------Alan Wilder
```

Director ------------------------------- Simon Curtis
Designer ------------------------------ Thomas Lynch

This production subsequently transferred to the Neil Simon Theatre on Broadway, on May 1, 1994 with the following cast:

```
MARI HOFF----------------------------Rondi Reed
LV ----------------------------------Hynden Walch
PHONE MAN -------------John Christopher Jones
BILLY ------------------------------- Ian Barford
SADIE ------------------------------- Karen Vaccaro
RAY SAY ----------------------------George Innes
MR BOO--------------------John Christopher Jones
```

Director ------------------------------- Simon Curtis
Designer ------------------------------ Thomas Lynch

CHARACTERS

MARI HOFF

LITTLE VOICE

PHONE MAN

BILLY

SADIE

RAY SAY

MR. BOO

MUSICIANS

TIME AND PLACE

A northern town in England.
The present.

THE RISE AND FALL OF LITTLE VOICE

ACT I

Darkness.
A long scream from MARI.

MARI. There's one. (*SHE screams again.*) There's another one. You scream.

LV. No.

MARI. No, you never scream, you hardly speak but you play your records, don't you?

LV. You're drunk, you.

(*In the BLACKNESS, we hear the sound of MARI smashing things around.*)

MARI. And you put out the damn stinking lights, don't you?

(*Suddenly LIGHTS COME UP and LV is at the fusebox on a chair. Record player in her room suddenly whirrs back into life very loud.*)

MARI. (*Almost falling over.*) Shut that up! Stop it! Get if off! Get it!

7

(LV runs upstairs fast. SHE gets in her room, takes it off. begins putting another one on.)

MARI. Come down.

(LV doesn't answer)

MARI. O'kay, stay up. Play your old records. Bore me. Make me want to be sick all over the house. *(Pause)*

MARI. Hey, hey, this better not cock up the putting in of my new phone tomorrow. It won't, will it?
LV. No.
MARI. Goodoh for that.

(LV puts on a different record. MARI stands in living room tottering. Suddenly, record from LV's room really loud. SHE turns, feels sick, suddenly rushes to kitchen sink. Retching but nothing happening. SHE slides and knocks all the pans and plates off the side. Collapses on the kitchen floor. LV comes running downstairs. MUSIC still playing loud. Helps MARI up. THEY stumble together. LV manages to get her back to the settee. THEY fall together on that. LV is trapped underneath her but manages to get out. SHE rolls her over on settee and tucks MARI'S coat around her, takes off MARI'S shoes, places them carefully. Cover's MARI'S ears with pillows Starts to go upstairs. MARI moans and mumbles. LV stops, turns back, then carries on up. LV goes in her room. Turns the record up even louder. Listens awhile. Bam. Electricity blows again.)

LV. Not again.

(BLACKOUT.

LIGHTS UP. Living room. Morning. A MAN and a very
tall younger man [Billy] from the phone company are
fitting in a phone. THEY have baggy overalls on.
MARI in dressing gown, watching them.)

MARI. Is it nearly in now?

PHONE MAN. Nearly in.

MARI. I'll be in touch with the world soon. I can't
believe it, I'll be wired up to all parts.

PHONE MAN. You will, love.

MARI. Goodly. I spend my life and my fortune in them
slot boxes, really I do.

(The PHONE MAN stands up.)

MARI. Oh, them uniforms are not very becoming. You
look like you've been thrown in a tool bag.

(PHONE MAN laughs.)

MARI. It's put me right off that. And I always liked a
man in uniform too.

PHONE MAN. I bet you did.

MARI. Eh, watch it Sparks, Sparkeler. Eh, speaking of
sparks, you don't know nothing about electrickery do you?
The wires of me home is crackling up on me.

PHONE MAN. No, I'm just a phone chap.

MARI. And a good un I hope. How we doing?

PHONE MAN. Almost there.
MARI. He's quiet in' he? (*Indicating tall one.*)
PHONE MAN. He is.
MARI. Is there anybody there? (*Laughs.*) Has he been disconnected? My daughter's like that.
PHONE MAN. Speak to her, Bill.
BILLY. Hi.
MARI. Eh, you're not the famous phone bill, are you?

(*THEY laugh.*)

MARI. I'm on form this morning, bloody Nora. I'm excited you see. Hey, don't think I'm tight or anything not offering tea, but you see how I want the job done as quick as possible don't you. I want voices. And also I'm expecting a call, if you know what I mean.

(*PHONE MAN laughs.*)

MARI. You do, don't you? Look at you though in that bag. You ought to complain. I might phone and complain for you. Good looking on the top, then that. Clark Gable in a bag, or should I say Clark Cable. (*SHE laughs, then suddenly sings, excited.*) "Oh, give me a phone where the phoneolohs phone." Hurry up, lads.

(*PHONE MAN hands BILLY a hammer. BILLY turns to put it in toolbag. LV enters from stairs. BILLY drops hammer. LV jumps.*)

BILLY. (*Shy.*) Sorry.

(THEY both bend to pick it up. SHE picks it up first, gives it to him, half smiles.)

MARI. Oh, look at them two looking now. Hey, he doesn't speak as well. You could go out together and have a silent night, holy night.

(LV goes back upstairs.)

MARI. Eh, what did I say? What did I say? And look at the red of him now, looky. Oh dear.

(Suddenly MUSIC comes on loud from upstairs.)

MARI. Hang on. *(SHE hits the ceiling with something.)* Cull it!

(The MUSIC goes down.)

MARI. That's all you get when she's upset, crappaty records, full blast.
PHONE MAN. Right madam, it's done, I'll just ring through to test the line.
MARI. Oh, let me. Let me, go on.
PHONE MAN. Okay. *(HE passes phone to her.)*
MARI. Oh, this virgin blower and coil, this spanking plastic, this phone of mine. Right, what's the number?
PHONE MAN. 76543
MARI. 7 ... Oh, you press, I'll dialogue.

(HE does, SHE speaks.)

MARI. Hiyah, love, we're on. Yes. Yes. Officer Phone said I could ring you. Bye-oh.

(SHE puts phone down. PHONE MAN holds out a sheet and a pen.)

PHONE MAN. Okay, could you sign this please. Er ...?

MARI. *(Takes sheet.)* Mrs. Hoff. Mari Hoff. *(As SHE takes pen.)* Crappaty name in' it? My late husband, Frank, left it me. *(As SHE signs.)* You can imagine my feelings on signing the marriage register, Mr. and Mrs. F. Hoff.

PHONE MAN. Aye. *(Laughs.)*

MARI. *(Picks up the phone again.)* See you now.

PHONE MAN. See you.

MARI. *(Dialling.)* Thank you Clark Cable, byeoh.

(THEY are leaving.)

BILLY. *(Quiet.)* See you.

(SHE ignores him. HE takes a last glance upstairs, leaves. LV enters down the stairs. Picks up newspapers. Heads for kitchen.)

LV. I hope you've paid for that.

MARI. Oh shut up, it's me new toy and in fact me lifeline. Okay? Live while you can, that's my motto and your lesson. Ring phone, ring.

(MARI puts phone down. LV is sitting at kitchen table.)

MARI. Shove us some food on something, LV. Go on, slap some food about for me, love. Come on.

LV. There is none.

MARI. Please don't tell me that. (*MARI gets up, goes to kitchen looking for food. SHE bangs her hand on kitchen table.*) Oh, you're a misery you. Buck up will you.

(*LV spills her drink, MARI returns to search.*)

MARI. What did you do last night?

(*LV doesn't answer.*)

MARI. Play your records. Play your records. Bloody shit. (*Goes searching for food.*) You wanna live a bit.

LV. Like you, you mean. The Merry Widow.

MARI. Can't hear you. You'll have to speak up, Little Voice. That's all we ever said when you was a kid. (*Still looking for food.*) No bacon? I can't start the day without some dribbling fat. Can you? What you eating, an old envelope?

LV. A Ryvita.

MARI. What, are you still a vegetarian?

(*LV nods.*)

MARI. Oh yes. I forgot. (*Still looking for food.*) I'll tell you what, if there was a squealer in here, I'd chop it meself. Cut, cut. (*SHE leaves kitchen, comes back into the living room.*) What's on the telly? (*Turns it on, turns it off before it even comes on.*) Oh sod that. Oh sod this, I'm going down the cafe. But first, ring, phone, ring. Give us paper while I'm waiting.

(LV passes it to her.)

MARI. *(Looks at her.)* Why are you so miserable?

(LV ignores her.)

MARI. Hey and listen you. I've been meaning to have a word with you for sometime about something. You never speak, right, you never leave the house. I want to know once and for all, are you agrophobical? Because if you are, you can get out.
LV. I'm not.
MARI. Eh? Right then. *(Reads on. Sits on sofa.)* Come on love, make us a cuppa.

(LV ignores her. MARI throws newspaper up in air.)

MARI. Bloody hell. Bloody hell, eh?

(KNOCK at door.)

MARI. Come in, Sadie.

(A great big fat WOMAN comes in. The neighbour.)

MARI. Sit down. Crush a chair anywhere you like.
SADIE. Okay.
MARI. Do you want a cuppa or 'owt?
SADIE. Okay.

MARI. Make us one while you're at it.

SADIE. Okay.

MARI. Where am I this morning, the Okay Corral or what? Frig me. Don't put loads of bloody sugar in yours an all. You emptied half the bloody bag yesterday. Do you like me phone?

SADIE. (*Looking*.) Okay that.

MARI. Okay! Wait 'til it start trilling. In fact we shouldn't have long to wait as I'm expecting a call this morning.

SADIE. (*Excited*.) A chap?

MARI. On the nail, Sade.

(*LV stands to leave.*)

MARI. Where you going?

(*LV just makes her way upstairs.*)

MARI. Don't start that bloody music again. I've no head for that. (*To Sadie*.) Can you hear it next door?

SADIE. At times, when I'm pegging out.

MARI. (*To LV*.) Did you hear that. (*To Sadie*.) Bloody crazed chil' she is. She bugs me at times. Though I'm all she's got and she's all I've got, besides me arse and tits. Where's that brew?

(*LV puts a recording on. It plays.*
MARI bangs a broomstick on the ceiling beneath LV's room.)

MARI. Cull it!

(LV turns it down. SHE gently puts her head on the player.)

MARI. I don't know what to do with her. She's morbidity itself, just plays them damn records her dad left her, over and a over. Just them, nothing else, on and on. That's not health is it, Sade? But what can I do? You can only do so much, can't you Sade?

(SADIE brings really steaming tea over.)

SADIE. You can. You said chap?
MARI. Oh yes ... yes. *(Takes tea.)* Tar. Let me see yours. *(SADIE shows.)* I can see the sugar! Will you stop that.
SADIE. Okay.
MARI. Go on, drink it now.

(THEY both sip.)

MARI. Well, Sadie, what a night! What-a-night! What a championship neet! I picked up that Ray again. I did it again! He had no choice. He motored me home about a million miles an hour, then screeching to a halt outside, did you not hear us? I saw every other curtain in the bitching road twitch. Then he comes at me with this pronto smooch, lip-lapping like hell. That's men for you in it Sade, if you can remember. At least he's a lot better than most, at least there's always the thick wad of his wallet up against your tit for comfort.
SADIE. Aye.

MARI. And he's got a finger in so many pies, Sadie. Some too hot for his own good if you get my meaning. In fact, he's moving into artist's management at the moment, you know. Yes. He's got a crooner, a dog act and two strippers at the moment. But he'll make it, he'll make it in anything, Ray Say. (*Sips.*) See, that's why I got the (*Indicating phone.*) ragbone in. I've got to be on call. It's got to be smooth for him going out with me. I must win him. I've got to keep him. He's got a lot of young bitches into him a quart my age. I know they haven't got my wizzle and mince but I'm taking no chances Sade, how can I at my time of strife?

(*MUSIC comes on loud again.*)

MARI. Oh trash that calypso!

(*It goes down again.*)

MARI. God I'm starving. I've got to eat if I'm gonna hold my own with him on the phone.

(*SADIE gets up to leave.*)

MARI. While you're at the door get me me coat.

(*SADIE does and holds it for her, MARI slips it on. SADIE goes out. MARI shouts upstairs.*)

MARI. I'm going down the cafe. If anyone phones before I return, this is more important than your life, girl,

tell them I'll be back in five minutes. Tell them that and
that's all, alright? ALRIGHT? Are you receiving me?

LV. (*From bedroom.*) Yes.

MARI. Toodle pip.

(*SHE leaves. The MUSIC is turned up full. LV emerges
from bedroom, comes downstairs. MUSIC playing
loud. SHE goes in kitchen. SHE opens fridge door,
looks in. Closes it. Fills and plugs kettle in. Goes and
picks pieces of newspaper up, tidies a little. PHONE
rings. SHE looks at it scared. Looks at it. Lowers her
hand over it. Retreats. Runs upstairs, turns off record
player. Peeps down, it's still ringing. Comes down,
frightened. Suddenly, a KNOCK at the door. SHE looks
at door. KNOCK again. SHE opens it. It is the shy
phone boy, BILLY.*)

BILLY. Hello, I put your phone in.

(*SHE nods.*)

BILLY. I think we left our hammer.

(*SHE looks, sees it, nods. Steps back to let him in.*)

BILLY. Oh. (*HE goes to get it. It's by the phone. HE
gets it.*) Your phone's ringing.

(*SHE nods. Looks at it. HE can see SHE's uncomfortable.*)

BILLY. Do you want me to get it for you?

(SHE nods. HE picks it up.)

BILLY. Er ... Mari ... Er ...
LV. She's gone Caf-Caf.
BILLY. What?
LV. Back soon.
BILLY. She will be back soon. Right. Right. *(Puts phone down.)* Ray, he'll ring back.
LV. Thanks.
BILLY. *(Clutching hammer.)* Yes. *(Not knowing what to say.)* I don't like talking on phones an' all. An' I work with 'em.

(SHE nods. THEY look at each other. HE wants to say more, but can't.)

BILLY. See you then. *(HE goes to leave. Stops.)* See you.

(LV nods. HE leaves. SHE closes door. KETTLE explodes. BLACKOUT.
LIGHTS UP.
Living room, night. LV is sitting in the DARK. TV on, LIGHT flickering up her face, an old film of one of her singer's is on.
Door suddenly bursts open. MARI there. Switches LIGHT on.)

MARI. Right you. You've got a fucking second to get in shape. *(Runs from back, leaps over the settee. Turns TV off. Goes back round towards door.)* Perk, girl,,, perk. *(At door.*) Aye come in Ray. Come in. Here he is (*SHE holds her hand towards door.*) Mr. Ray Say.

(*MAN comes in, forties, in a suit, hair quiffed slightly.*)

MARI. Here it is, my home. My phone. My kitchen. My wall. My telly. My daughter.

RAY. How do.

MARI. Ray. Sun Ray. Sting Ray. Ray Gun. My Ray of hope. I'm a frigging just inta him so. (*SHE kisses him. To LV.*) Well, say hello at least. You miserable spot. I've warned you.

LV. (*Awkwardly, almost inaudible.*) Hello.

MARI. Oh, she's a miserable misery. What you having Raymondo and don't say nowt rude, ha!

RAY. What's in?

MARI. Everything your throat could desire. (*SHE suddenly speeds to one place and gathers up an armful of bottles, too many to hold properly, and places them down on the table. Backs off.*) There.

RAY. I'll have a cup of tea, tar.

MARI. You'll what? He'll have a cup o'tea. Har. He ha he. (*Looks at LV.*) Look, look she nearly laughed then, din't you eh? Nearly.

(*LV stands up and heads for her bedroom.*)

MARI. Hey, don't just go like that, you rude slit. Hey!

RAY. Leave her, she's alright.

MARI. No. It's not right, she spoils everything, her. I'm trying to make an impression and she can't even be swivel to a friend. The little tiny slit! (*SHE kicks a chair over, boots the bottles.)* Oh what am I doing and in front of you! Oh well, that's it, I give up. This is my crappaty home, and this is how I am, Ray, no gracey airs, and if you don't like it piss off out of it.

RAY. Hey, hey, calm down. Don't get mad at me. I didn't say anything about anything.

MARI. Oh, okay, come on, let's roll about.

(SHE pulls him on settee. His drink goes flying. THEY snog and roll about. Suddenly, from above, loud MUSIC from LV's record player.)

RAY. What's up?
MARI. I'll shut her up.
RAY. Leave it.

(MARI hits ceiling again.
The music doesn't go down. Angry. SHE starts to go upstairs.)

MARI. Right!
RAY. Hey, hey never mind. Come on. Come here.
MARI. *(Stops.)* Ha. You're right. Sod the bitch. We'll have our own on.

(SHE goes to radiogram, puts her own record on. Turns it up. Both are going now. SHE goes back to Ray. THEY roll about snogging. Suddenly the LIGHTS go. The electricity has gone again. RAY stops. The two record players grind to a halt.)

MARI. You've blown me fuse.

(THEY laugh and carry on. LV begins singing. It sounds just like the record. RAY and MARI snogging. Then suddenly RAY stops.)

RAY. How can that be, has she a radio?

MARI. That's not "her," that's her.

RAY. What?

MARI. I mean, that's not the record, that's LV.

RAY. No.

MARI. Yeah.

RAY. No.

MARI. Yeah.

RAY. No.

MARI. Fucking hell.

RAY. That's her singing, but that's amazing.

MARI. Amazin' Ray sin. Come on, let's roll about.

RAY. Hold on. How can she do that?

MARI. I don't know, throat twisting, I presume. Roll.

RAY. I still don't believe it.

MARI. Look, Ray, she plays 'em all the time, every God sented sec'. They're stuck in her head. She can sing them. It gets on my wick. End of story. Come on. I'm ready.

RAY. Where did she get them?

MARI. When he died, he left them her.

RAY. Your husband?

MARI. Yeah, Frank.

RAY. What was he like then?

MARI. Put it this way, he listened to women's records.

RAY. So.

MARI. Put it this way. He was thin and tall and hardly spoke. When I was a teenager, I thought I'd found Gary Cooper but ended up I'd found Olive Oil. He was a length of dry stick that bored me bra-less. He sat folded up in that chair there resembling misery in its many fucking forms and he tried to make me the same. He could not succeed. Come on lover boy.

RAY. (*Still towards the singing.*) Hang on, I'm listening.

MARI. Come on, lover boy, I'm contorted here.

RAY. Ssssh. Hold on.

MARI. Oh, I'm off then.

(*SHE closes her eyes and immediately falls asleep. RAY listens intently till the song ends. Then HE starts clapping.*
LV, upstairs, afraid.
BLACKOUT.
Living room/kitchen morning.
LV comes downstairs, goes in kitchen. Opens bread bin. Takes out a curled crust of white bread from the bottom of it. SHE is heading for toaster with it. RAY appears from stairs, pulling on Mari's dressing gown over bare chest and trousers.)

RAY. Hi.

(*SHE drops the precious piece of bread.*)

RAY. Don't get a shock, it's only me, Ray Say, remember.

*(SHE doesn't speak, goes to plug in kettle. It flashes. SHE
    jumps again.)*

RAY. You wanna watch that. Could fetch the house
down. And so could you with what you did last night.

(LV retreats further into kitchen. Gets a glass of water.)

RAY. Bloody marvellous that. Who else do you do, eh?

(SHE starts to go.)

RAY. Don't go. I'm interested 'cause I'm show
business meself you see. R. Say very personal
management. Your Mam must have told you. No? Well
never mind. *(Indicating bread.)* Shame about the crust
cocker, here let me rustle you up one of Ray Say's famous
breakfassays. I do 'em all the time for my artistes, when
we's on a foreign engagement. Not all glamour our game
you know. *(HE opens fridge.)* Oh God. *(Closes it quick.)*
You ever bin to Spain?
LV. No.
RAY. Last weekend I flew a couple of the girls and
myself out to do a show. I know an old jockey runs a
bartello there, "The Princess Di," good gig, good gig.
Bloody mad out there though. Raging love, wild. Not like
the postcards. I've got two scars somewhere I brought back
for souvenirs. One on me chest, see. And one on me lip,
look. *(HE gets close, SHE looks.)* Can I just say again
while you're this close. Bloody marvellous what you did
last night. Marvellous in the dark there, something I'll
never forget. Do you mind if I ask you something, love?

(LV shakes her head.)

RAY. How the hell on earth do you do it?

LV. Uh, I ...

RAY. No, no don't try. Don't. You wouldn't know. The true performer never does, take it from me. I understand the artiste, you see. (*HE casually pulls a packet of cornflakes down, looks in.*) What's this, a box of privet leaves, urgh, they's all green. (*HE puts them back.*) I'll tell you what, what say you and me continue our conversation down the cafe.

LV. No.

RAY. (*Surprised.*) No ... I'll pay and everything. (*Gets his fat wallet out.*)

LV. No.

RAY. Okay, suit yourself.

LV. But.

Ray Yeah.

LV. Er ...?

RAY. Hey fire away, love.

LV. In show business, did you ever meet Shirley Bassey?

RAY. Now then, Shirley, to be honest no, love, our paths have never crossed. I've met Monkhouse though. (*Sees SHE's not impressed.*) And of course, Lulu.

LV. Lulu?

RAY. Yeah.

LV. No.

RAY. Sure.

LV. (*Eager.*) What's she like?

RAY. Alreet.

LV. I've got one of hers upstairs.
RAY. You can't do her an' all can you?

(HE starts putting his wallet away [or any action here that will serve as a distraction for him]. While he's distracted and not looking SHE sings in Lulu's voice.)

LV. "Weellllll, you know you make me want to shout." *(Snaps straight back to her normal expression, almost completely unaware of what she has done.)*

(RAY turns.)

RAY. *(Seriously shocked.)* Christ, I can't believe that. Take it from me. Hey ... Hey. Honest, love. Take it from me ... Does no one know about this?
LV. No. *(Shakes her head.)*
RAY. I can't believe it. What does your Mam say?
LV. Nowt.
RAY. Nowt?
LV. No.
RAY. Listen seriously, LV. Listen, you are my discovery. I've found you right, me, always remember that. In fact, here, have one o' me new cards. *(HE gets one out.)* Gold, look.

(SHE is fascinated by the glint of it, but won't take it.)

RAY. No, here you are, you're the first to have one a these.

(SHE almost takes it, but doesn't.)

RAY. No, there, love. I wouldn't give one a these to everyone.

(SHE takes it.)

RAY. Now listen, LV. I know you're quiet, your mam's told me that, but together you and me we could set the place on fire.
LV. You're a nutter you. *(SHE goes.)*
RAY. And you're a star.

(SHE goes upstairs.
RAY, excited, runs to phone. Dials.)

RAY. Hello! Hello, is Mr. Boo in, I need to speak to him now ... It's Ray Say, Say, Say. Yeah. No, it can't wait, no. Hold him there. I'm coming down now!

(HE puts phone down, starts off upstairs to finish dressing. Half way up HE meets MARI coming down, looking rough.)

RAY. Marrii!
MARI. Don't speak to me. Don't speak for a minute.

(RAY laughs and continues upstairs.
MARI comes down. SHE goes in kitchen area hunting for something. Knocks something off draining board.)

MARI. Aarrrgh! *(Finds a bottle in the cupboard. Takes a big drink from it.)*

(RAY reappears, bounding downstairs, putting on tie. Jacket over arm.

MARI. *(Revived.)* Darling, how are you?

(Goes to embrace him. RAY is dressing as HE speaks.)

RAY. I've got to dash, Mari. But what can I say? It's happened at last, eh! I'm so excited, it's like at the races when you've found yourself a little nag no one's noticed but you know you're onto a certainty and you're feeling this is it! She is the one. Do you know what I mean?

(A KNOCK at the door.)

MARI. Go on, yes! Yes! I'm with you, lad. Yes ...
RAY. It's like ...
MARI. Yeah, Yeah. *(Desperate.)* Ignore that.

(It's too late, RAY is opening it. It's BILLY.)

BILLY. It's, er, me again. Er, just come to see if your phone's still alright.

(MARI snatches handset up. Holds it out to him.)

MARI. Is that its sound?
BILLY. Yes.
MARI. It's reet then!

(Slams door.)

MARI. On Ray, on.

RAY. (*Forgetting where he was.*) Er ...

MARI. You were under starters orders and you were off!

RAY. Yah. It's not just my future, it's yours.

MARI. Oh my God.

RAY. I still can't believe it. It's what I've been looking for for ages. And here it is under this roof, under me very nose. All I can say is ...

(*KNOCK on door. RAY opens it.*)

MARI. No, leave it! For Godsake leave it!

(*SADIE is standing there.*)

RAY. (*As HE leaves.*) I'll be back soon. I can't leave it. Not this. Best to act fast when you're this sure, eh?

(*MARI nods frantically.*)

RAY. It's just one o'them once in a lifetime things.

(*HE passes SADIE and leaves. MARI takes her by the sleeve and silently draws her in the house.*)

MARI. Sadie, did you hear that utterance? Did you? Did you hear what Say sayeth. It were almost on the tip there of his raspberry tongue, he wants me I can't believe it, Sade. The bastard wants me. Get "our song" on, Sadie. We always play it when we've something to celebrate, don't we?

(SADIE, happy, runs to radiogram and gets it on.)

MARI. At last. At last. Saved, secured. I shall go to the ball. Oh darlings from the sky.

(The MUSIC comes on. THEY dance all around the room. MUSIC blaring. THEY dance till they have to stop.)

MARI. Oh, oh stop. I can't breathe.

(SADIE turns it off. THEY collapse on settee and chairs.)

MARI. Din't I say to you though, Sadie, when I first spied him, I knew there was summat down for us. I just had that twat-bone feeling, and you know me, I can predict rain with that. (*SHE suddenly gets up.*) Hey, I'd better get dressed up, who knows when he will return. Where's me knickers and bra?

(Pulls some out the washing basket, THEY are all tangled up with a line of other bras and knickers and suspender belts and tea towels, etc. SHE can't separate them.)

MARI. (*Speaking as SHE tries.*) I'm one high razzamatazza in here today. (*Hitting her chest.*) It's like there's a circus parade passing over my paps. What a life, life can be.

(In the end SHE just takes them all up in a long trail. SHE heads for the stairs trailing them all behind her.)

MARI. (*As SHE ascends.*) Sadie, make yourself a cup of sugar with some tea in it. I shall be down shortly.

(*SHE goes upstairs and into her room, slams door. SADIE, still panting, goes into kitchen to make tea.*
LV alone in her room. Suddenly, we see a yellow "Cherry Picker" [Platform on a winch, used by telephone engineers and for lighting maintenance on lamp-posts, etc.] coming high round the side of house. BILLY is in it, holding a hammer. It comes along alley and up level with her window. LV screams. BILLY speaks.)

BILLY. Just seeing if wires are alright.

(*SHE looks at him amazed. Can't hear him through the window.*)

BILLY. (*Louder.*) Just seeing if wires are alright!

(*SHE opens window.*)

BILLY. Just seeing! ... (*Nearly knocks her over with shout, quickly quietens.*) ... if wires are alright. (*Starts whistling. Presses button, goes out to side a bit, away from her view. Whistling as HE looks at wall, up and down.*) Do you get out much?
LV. No.

(*BILLY whistling.*
Whistling trails off.)

BILLY. There are no wires.

LV. Eh?

BILLY. I should be up a telephone pole three streets away, but I come here.

(Presses button, returns to window.
THEY look at each other.)

BILLY. I don't know what to say now.

(Pause. THEY look at each other.)

BILLY. I'm like this at work. Then when I do speak they all jump like I've dropped a brick in a bucket.

(HE smiles nervously. SHE does a little.)

BILLY. I'm Billy. Can I ask you your name.
LV. LV.
BILLY. Oh, does that stand for something?
LV. Little Voice.
BILLY. Oh, 'cause of your soft voice.
LV. I think it's more 'cause no one could never hear me.
BILLY. I can.

(Pause.)

BILLY. Your mam's a live wire in't she. Bloody hell.
LV. Aye.
BILLY. I live with me grandad. It's quiet in our house, the clock an' all that.
LV. Ours is a mad house.

BILLY. Aye. (*Pause.*) Hope you don't mind having a chat this high up.

LV. No, do you?

BILLY. No. No. Safe as houses these. It goes higher than this, this. See. (*HE presses a button. Machine rises to above the roof height.*) I like going up. Better view.

LV. What view?

BILLY. (*Looking.*) Backs. Backs. Works. Works. Backs. Works. Backs. And the last chimney.

LV. I can't even see that.

BILLY. No, your view's blocked by the factory.

LV. Me Mam works there.

BILLY. Oh, aye. Maybe I can see her through one of the little windows.

LV. You won't. She hardly ever goes in.

BILLY. Oh.

(*HE presses button, comes down. LV stands up. THEY face each other.*)

BILLY. Little Voice, I don't know what's come over me. I've not been able to rest till I could come here again. I've only been like this once before. That's when I first saw Blackpool illuminations. (*Pause.*) Do you by any chance, like, by any chance, light displays at all LV? I only ask 'cause it's the one thing I can really talk about and I don't want to dry up on you, not now.

(*SHE smiles, confused. HE takes this as permission to continue.*)

BILLY. I've got me grandad's shed and I've blacked out the windows. I ... No, I'll say no more, it can be boring to the non-enthusiast.

LV. No, go on.

BILLY. You sure.

(LV nods.)

BILLY. Inside that shed. Inside that shed. When I throw the switch, Little Voice, you wouldn't believe it. Lights. Up the walls. Off the ceiling. Caught light, bent light, beams under beams of it, colours, colours coming up through colours you've never seen. Shades to make you happy, shades to make you sad, shades to make you *voom!*

(The last word HE sent out so powerfully in his excitement, LV falls back in surprise.)

BILLY. Sorry!

LV. No.

BILLY. So sorry.

LV. It's alright.

BILLY. I don't know what it is, after the illuminations, that was it. I'd only play with torches and Christmas tree lights, I spent all me youth with the curtains closed, fascinated, helpless as a moth. *(Pause.)* Only thing is I'll never show. Me grandad says I'm like an artist painting masterpieces and keeping them under the stairs, he keeps pestering me to do the lights for his pensioners' dance down at the workingmen's club. I always say no. Somehow though, I don't know. After talking to you, telling you. Maybe I shall do it. I don't know. If I did would you come down?

LV. I don't know. I don't go out.

BILLY. Would you think about it. I could go and find out all the details. I really would be honoured. I really would be so ... If you could just see them, LV. (*Almost to himself.*) I'd take from above, I'd bring down some heaven. Poor old sods they'd think they were getting a mirror ball and a couple of spotlights and they'd be flying when I'd done.

(*MARI comes out of her bedroom, stops on landing.*)

MARI. What's going on. You talking to yourself now, gal!

LV. (*To Billy.*) Sorry. I got go. (*SHE hurriedly pulls curtain across open window.*)

MARI. Is that you and your voices?

BILLY. LV, the lights.

(*LV is gone inside. HE presses button, begins to disappear back round corner.*)

MARI. (*To herself.*) Crazed.

(*MARI comes grandly downstairs, tarted up. SADIE is in living room.*)

MARI. Well, Sadie, how do I look? And don't say okay or I'll poke your Pillsbury dough.

(SADIE has a mouthful of something, so just nods approvingly.)

MARI. What you eating? I thought there was nothing in.

SADIE. Cornflakes.

MARI. Oh.

(Suddenly, the sound of a CAR outside screeching up. MARI looks out of window.)

MARI. It's Ray Say. I didn't expect him so soon. *(SHE rushes to mirror; lacquer can and sherry bottle at side. Starts lacquering and quick drinking in turn.)* Lacquer! Liquor! Lacquer! Liquor! *(SHE lacquers all over he hair and everywhere fast.)* Oh I've had the colour shocked out of me. *(Slaps both her cheeks hard.)* Come on up you young apples. You cheeky cheeks. *(SHE looks out again.)* He's got someone wi' him. Maybe it's the vicar.

(SADIE stands up.)

MARI. Don't take me serious, Sade. *(To herself.)* Fat sucker.

(SADIE sits again.)

MARI. No, no it's that bloke from the club, what the hell's he doing with him? Come on, Sadie, sod off. I need some seats free. *(Changing her mind.)* No, no stay and get drinks.

(KNOCK at door. MARI opens it. RAY and MR. BOO step in.)

MARI. Darling, din' expect you back so swoon.

RAY. Mari, you know Mr. Boo from down the club.

MR. BOO. Call me Lou.

MARI. *(Almost curtseying.)* Pleasured I'm sure, Mr. Lou.

RAY. No, Lou's his first name.

MARI. *(Almost curtseying again.)* Sorry. Sit down.

RAY. This is Little Voice's mother.

MARI. *(To Ray.)* Hang on. Little Voice? What's going on?

RAY. Like I said Mari, LV's a real discovery, a once in a lifetime thing. That's why I've dragged Mr. Boo straight down here to hear her.

(MR. BOO nods.)

MARI. LV?

RAY. Yeah.

(SHE goes away to her liquor bottle by mirror.)

RAY. Will you just get her down for us, cock, Mr. Boo's not got long you see, have you?

Mr. BOO. *(Looking at watch.)* Nope.

MARI. *(Drinking.)* You know where she rots. Fetch her yourself.

(RAY goes upstairs a little.)

RAY. (*Softly.*) LV! LV! It's Ray Say, remember? Can you come down, love. I've brought someone to hear you do your stuff, love?

(*MR. BOO coughs.*)

RAY. Someone important LV, love!

(*No response. HE goes right up to Mari.*)

RAY. Mari, will you go and get her?

MARI. (*Snaps at Ray.*) You're tapped, you. She'll not sing in public, LV.

RAY. Hey, I want Boo to hear her sing, alright?

MARI. She'll not throat on cue, LV.

MR. BOO. Everything alright, Say?

RAY. Oh aye.

MR. BOO. Just reminding you, lad, I've not all day.

RAY. Aye. (*To Mari.*) Listen, my reputation's at stake here, get up them dancers and get her down.

MARI. Easier said than done.

RAY. Listen, Mari, I want her down. What's up with you?

MARI. You.

RAY. Eh?

MARI. You with your "special" and all that, the "one and only" and all that. I thought you meant me din't I?

RAY. (*Struggling now.*) Hey. I do. Bloody hell, Mari, I did. I do. Yes. You are special, bloody hell, you know that. I meant I found you both at the same time. That's what I meant. Eh? 'Course I did. (*Puts his arm around her.*) Eh?

MARI. Oooh you.

(MARI goes up close to RAY, almost kissing.)

MARI. Elvis breath.
RAY. Go on, get her down, love.
MARI. Well, anything for you love, but I think you've backed your first loser there, Ray, sorry to say.

(SHE goes to stairs. Stops on first step, looks over to SADIE and MR. BOO. MR. BOO reading newspaper. SADIE staring out.)

MARI. Sadie talk to Lou Boo. *(Carries on upstairs to LV's room.)*
SADIE. Okay. *(To Mr. Boo.)* Hello.
MR. BOO. Hi.

(SADIE just turns back to looking out. MR. BOO glares over at Ray.)

RAY. *(To Mr. Boo.)* Won't be a minute now Mr. Boo.

(MR. BOO cracks out the paper and reads again.)

MARI. LV. LV.

(LV is inside, album covers all around her. SHE has one up in front of her face as SHE reads the back of it. It has a lifesize face of the singer on it, taking the place of LV's face.)

MARI. Come down, Ray wants you a minute.

(SHE doesn't reply.)

MARI. Ray wants you for a minnesota, will you get down?

LV. What for?

MARI. You know what for, you've got him thinking you can do summat or summat. He wants you down anyway, show some showman or summat.

LV. It's private.

MARI. Private, my privates. You're just damn selfish and useless and can do nowt but whisper and whine like your father before you, a couple of nowts. *(LV turns away, behind record sleeve.)* A load of dirty auld discs and a clapped out player. The sum of your father's life. Just a load of old rubbish nobody wants.

(LV covers her ears. MARI snatches LP cover from her. LV gets it back.)

LV. Don't dare ever touch these.

MARI. Up yours, stick leg. *(SHE goes out and downstairs to Ray. On her way down.)* She won't come down.

RAY. What?

MARI. Just as I told you, she won't sing, told you.

Mr. BOO. What's happening, Say?

RAY. She's not quite prepared yet, Mr. Boo, late sleeper and all that, see.

MR. BOO. Well, I've gotta be off. Sorry and all that, Say. Maybe some other time, eh.

RAY. Hold on.

MR. BOO. (*To Sadie.*) Goodbye er ...

SADIE. Sadie May.

MR. BOO. Sadie May, nice to make your acquaintance. Bye all.

(Starts to leave. RAY goes after him.)

RAY. Mr. Boo wait. I'm sure we can persuade her. Hold on, give me a minute. I'll get her down. Believe me, Boo! It's like I said.

(MR. BOO's out. RAY's out after him. MARI follows on. SADIE after. DOOR slams.)

MR. BOO. Hard to tell when I've heard nowt.

MARI. Leave it, Ray.

RAY. (*To Mr. Boo.*) Come back inside.

MR. BOO. Enough's enough. I've got to get back down to the club.

RAY. Look, you know me. I wouldn't fetch you down here for nowt. You've got to hear her. I can sort it, you know me.

(LV upstairs has heard the door slam, thinking she's alone, SHE sits on her bed, sings to herself.
Suddenly VOICES outside subside to silence. MR. BOO appears and stands under lamp-post.
RAY comes next and joins him. Then MARI and last, SADIE. THEY cluster under the lamp, almost like carol singers, listening. SHE sings a couple of verses. Stops.)

RAY. That was her.
MR. BOO. Wasn't.
RAY. Was.
MR. BOO. Wasn't.
RAY. Was.
MR. BOO. No.
RAY. Yes.
MARI. (*To herself.*) Here we fucking go again.

(LV starts to sing again, another song, sings some, then hums softly.)

RAY. That was her an all.

MR. BOO. Well, it's remarkable that. You have a remarkable daughter there, Mrs. Hoff.

MARI. Thank you, I'm sure.

MR. BOO. Well, Ray, we must have her if you can arrange it. There's the makings of a class act there, class. We could do a lot with that.

RAY. It'll cost you.

MR. BOO. I expected it to.

RAY. Come on, Mr. Boo.

(THEY start to leave.)

RAY. (*To Mari.*) We're off to talk fine details and finances.

MARI. (*Following.*) I'm with you. Don't forget me. The flesh and blood management.

(LV picks up song again.

SADIE left standing alone below lamp, cheeks on hands,
   rapt. LV finishes song, totally unaware of what's taking
   place.
BLACKOUT.)

END OF ACT I

ACT II

The club.
The ORGAN and DRUMS duo are playing frantically away
at full blast.
MR. BOO comes on, the MUSIC stops with a
CYMBALS CLASH.

MR. BOO. Tar. Thank you. Tar. (*Indicates organist.*)
Jean on her organ, ladies and gentlemen, Jean.

(*MR. BOO applauds. JEAN plays a riff.*)

MR. BOO. Jean, lovely. And Manolito, ladies and
gentlemen, Manolito.

(*HE plays a bit of drums. MR. BOO applauds, riff*
continues as HE speaks.)

MR. BOO. Yes. Yes. Beat that meat, Manolito. Yes
sir. Bad man, bad.

(*HE does a little Michael Jackson dance. MANOLITO ends*
riff. MR. BOO steps forward to audience.)

MR. BOO. Yes. Here we are. Here we are then. (*MR.*
BOO at mike.) Boo Here. Don't shout my name too loud
or I'll think you don't like me. How you all doing, alreet?!
(*Waits for audience response.*) Come on you can do better

45

than that. How you all doing?! Alreet. Great. Now then, now then, as you know, Boo braves anything, goes anywhere in his perpetual quest to hunt down fresh talent and lay it at your mercy. And you know how I've sweated, and you know how I've toiled, and you know how I've bent over backwards. (*To someone in audience.*) Watch it! And you know I've left no tonsil unturned in my unceasing search for something new on the vocal front. But for all that, I've found her round the corner, on the doorstep, at the kitchen table, she's so local I could spit and hit her. A talent, an undiscovered treasure. An act of wonder, ladies and gentlemen, something to thrill to, to spill beer or tears to, a little girl that's big, a northern light, a rising star, order and hush, hush and order, for the turn of turns. The one, the only, LITTLE VOICE! LITTLE VOICE!

(*SPOTLIGHT burning the stage. Microphone on stand. RAY brings LV halfway on, directs her towards microphone, leaves. SHE comes into SPOT. Stands there. Quiet. Stands there. Quiet, trembling. Opens her mouth. Nothing. Upset.*)

RAY'S VOICE. Lights, turn the lights out!

(*All the LIGHTS go out. SHE sings.*
Perfect impersonation. After a few lines, suddenly stops abruptly.)

RAY'S VOICE. Do another, do another, more.
LV. (*Spoken. Judy Garland impersonation.*) I know ... I ... I'll sing 'em all, and we'll be here all night. (*SHE sings*

again. Another perfect impersonation. SHE stops abruptly.)

RAY'S VOICE. What you stopped for? Don't stop now. Do anything, anything.

(SHE sings again, another song. Stops.)

RAY'S VOICE. Get 'em back up! Back up!

(LIGHTS UP. SHE is caught "feeling it" then stunned like a frightened animal caught in headlights.
BLACKOUT.
LIGHTS UP. BAM.
Back at house. LV in her room. MARI downstairs, going frantically about the place throwing things over her shoulder, looking for something.
RAY at table, paper and pen out, working excitedly.)

MARI. Embarrassing!

(Throws something without looking. It just misses RAY, who doesn't even respond, just ducks and carries on working.)

MARI. Bloody one hundred chunk embarrassing that. I'm shown up. I'll never place my face in there again. Never, never. (*To Ray.*) Will you stop that scritching. I've just been involved with the worst spectacle and frig-up in Mari's history and you're crouched there scritching like a rat.

RAY. I'm working on the act.

MARI. Working on the act. Working on the act. Are you mental altogether? What act! There was only one sucker on show there tonight, me! Embarrassing. See her quavering in the dark there like a demic! See her! And what was she singing? What the hell was that? She could a made an effort and done Madonna for Christsake.

RAY. Calm down.

MARI. Calm down! You must be jesting. I'm up to me neck in shame.

RAY. We had to find her limits. See what she could do.

MARI. Nowt.

RAY. No. The gold's there alright. I've just got to find me a way of fetching it out.

MARI. Frig that. (*Returns to searching.*) Is there not a bottle nowhere?

RAY. If the artiste won't go to the act, the act will have to go to the artiste. All's I have to do is think. Get my mind out, think.

MARI. You should a thunk before. You wouldn't listen, would you? I told you and bloody Boo Lou, both, you were wasting your time on the slit. She did the whole thing on purpose to spite mother. I know her, Ray. Oh my God, when she come on like that, though. Oh my God. I din't know where to put meself. I still don't. Shame ran right up me leg.

(*Suddenly there's a sound like stones hitting a window. We see BILLY in the alley under the lamp, tossing little stones up to LV's window.*)

MARI. What's that? Is that in my head or on the outside?

RAY. Eh? What? (*HE listens.*) Outside.

MARI. Bam me, funny business! (*SHE bursts out of the house and sees BILLY.*) Clear off. Go on. Heated up pole. Piss it. Go.

(*HE's gone. SHE throws stones after him. MARI goes back in.*)

MARI. I'm too mad to live tonight.

(*SHE looks this way and that for something to grab. SHE turns on RAY who's still working.*)

MARI. Anyway, stop that off! 'Cause she's not doing another. No way. Don't forget that's my diddy and delicate daughter you're twiddling wi'. And besides that there's my personal mother's nerves to consider.

(*HE grabs her quickly by the wrist and pulls her onto his knee.*)

RAY. (*Quickly.*) Come here. Calm down! (*HE starts tickling her up and down.*) Calm down. Calm down.

(*SHE starts hooting and laughing.*)

MARI. Stop it. Ooooo. Stop it.
RAY. (*Tickling on.*) You're calming down now, eh? Calming down now, eh?

(*HE stops. SHE remains on his lap.*)

RAY. You calmed down now, eh? Eh?

MARI. Oh but Ray, it were crap awful weren't it, and you're on about putting us through it again.

RAY. Mari, it's there, believe me. She's not a performer, I'll admit, no, but I can take care of that. Bear with me, dove, while I work out the last details. I'm only gripping on to it so tight Mari, so pit bull tight, for all of us, 'cause I know it can take us to the top.

MARI. Oooh. I love it when you talk swanky.

RAY. If you knew how long I've been looking for summat like this. And here it is in me lap. (*Quickly*.) Along with you, along with you.

(SHE giggles and buries her head in him. As SHE does HE quickly writes more on the paper.)

RAY. Aye. Aye.

MARI. (*Comes back up.*) You really is gone on this, ain't you Ray?

RAY. I am, dove, I've never had nowt decent to set meself on before, scrap, bent bookying, a bit o' this and that, clapped out old acts and knackered strippers.

MARI. Don't. Don't do yoursen down, Ray. You're Elvis in my eyes.

RAY. Okay, granted, I might be the King of this gutter in which we live. But what's that? There's stuff above, love. Bungalows, gravel drives, Chateau Niff on tap, teeing off with Tarbuck and Brucie.

MARI. Ooooh, hey. (*Sings*.) I did it my Ray. Oh there were times, I've had a few, bit off, bit off ...

RAY. Aye, aye, Mari. (*Shoving her off his lap*.) I've just got make a quick call.

MARI. (*Stands up.*) Okay, man o'mine, frigging go for it and you can depend on me, one hundred pesetas. In fact, I'll drink to that. (*SHE goes off, still singing to herself, hunting for booze.*)

RAY. (*Into the phone.*) Hello. Hello. Tape-deck, is that you? Yep, it's Ray. I'm calling in that favour you owe me ...

(*MARI is still singing and chucking stuff about at the back.*)

RAY. (*Covers phone.*) Mari, Mari. Here, look, here. (*Holding out a fiver.*) Go and buy a bottle.

MARI. Ray, you're speaking my very language again. Tar. (*SHE takes it, tries kissing him, phone wire getting caught up, etc.*)

RAY. (*Pulling away.*) Aye.

MARI. See you later, Ray-ver.

RAY. Aye. Aye.

MARI. (*Leaving, stops at open door for an exit line. Overcome.*) Sometimes, suddenly, life's nothing but holy in' it?

(*SHE goes. Pause. RAY remains, looking at closed door in disbelief. Then turns back out front.*)

RAY. (*To himself.*) Bloody hell. (*Back on phone.*) Meet me tomorrow down the club, okay. Bring your stuff. Just be there.

(*Puts phone down. Carries on scribbling. BILLY appears in alley again, with a lamp, and shines light up into*

LV's room, turning it on and off. LV comes to window. Opens it to see what's outside.)

BILLY. Over here. It's me.

LV. Eh?

BILLY. Billy. LV, I've just been down the club after hours, to weigh up the space an all that. I got a shock. I saw "Little Voice" on a turn poster, singing impressionist. Is it you?

LV. You have lights. I have voices.

BILLY. Voices?

LV. I sing in these voices. I ... I hardly know I do it. It's just for me. Comfort. I ... I ...

BILLY. Hey, say no more, LV. That's enough for me. I understand. But why you doing it down there?

LV. They made me.

BILLY. Who made you?

LV. Him and her. They go on until you do.

BILLY. Can't you say 'owt to make them see?

LV. No one never listens to anybody but themselves, too loud.

BILLY. I do.

LV. Yes.

BILLY. Are they trying to make you do it again?

LV. She didn't like it. I won't be doing it no more.

BILLY. Oh well, that's good in it?

(SHE nods.)

BILLY. You do what's right for you, Little Voice.

(SHE nods.)

BILLY. And cheer up.

(SHE smiles.)

LV. Talk about the lights.

BILLY. Well, space down there is big enough. And it got me going. Aye, me brain came on straight away, making lights. Having a do wi' the dark. (*As though he's in the space.*) I thought, here, fwun. (*HE swings his torch out over the audience in a beam of LIGHT.*) There, (*Swings beam in another direction, across audience, making a sound like a bullet.*) pkooo. (*Another direction.*) Here, zhum. (*Stops.*) I saw all sorts. It'll take some time, though ... to fix it all up. Bloke said I can make a start any night as long as it's after hours. I don't know, though. Would you be coming down? You never said you see.

LV. I ... (*SHE hears footsteps on stairs.*)

BILLY. What's up?

LV. Oo somebody's coming. I got go now, will you come again, Billy?

BILLY. Yeah soon, soon as I can.

(RAY knocks on door. Goes in.)

RAY. LV, I've worked out the new act. You'll love it. Everything tailored to your personality. All you have to do is step on from the side.

(SHE looks away.)

RAY. What's the matter? Hey, don't let a little hiccup like tonight put you off. Could happen to anyone.

LV. Don't want do another.

RAY. Listen, could happen to the best of them that. (*Pointing at albums.*) If you could ask her or her or her they'd tell you the same. They've had them nights an' all. Haven't you, Judy? (*Answering in her voice.*) "I sure have Mr. Say." (*Laughs.*) How about you, Marilyn? "Yes Ray, boo be do."

LV. Don't.

RAY. Seriously, it'll never happen again, not with this LV. (*Showing paper.*) It's foolproof. Believe me. Let's do it, eh?

(LV shakes her head.)

RAY. Won't you even look at it?

(LV shakes her head.)

RAY. Well, if that's what you want. (*Folds paper in half.*)

LV. 'Tis.

RAY, Okay. But it's a shame to just leave it like that. How about just giving it a try, just once LV. (*Holds up a digit.*) One more time and if it don't work out we'll forget it forever. I'll leave you to your records and your room.

(SHE shakes her head. RAY folds paper again.)

RAY. Fair enough, I've got me other acts, I'll be alright. I'll survive, so will you, it's just that ... (*Looks at folded paper*.) Well never mind. Never mind then. That's that. (*HE folds paper completely and puts it in his back pocket*.) Aye, you've got it nice in here ain't you? Clean and tidy. (*Sits on her bed*.) All your records round you. (*Looks*.) You dad must a spent years building up this collection.

LV. He did.

RAY. I were never one for collecting things myself, only debts, I had an auntie who was though. You'll never guess what she collected, go on.

LV. What?

RAY. Bluebirds. Wild bluebirds. Flying all round her house. Marvellous with 'em she was. You know she even got one of 'em to talk once. Yeah. Timid little thing it was, no bigger than your thumb, too scared to even leave its cage. And the way she did it were so simple. All she did was keep it shaded and safe at all times, sing to it, while stroking it, very soft, every day. And after a while it gave her its heart. And later, when it had grown strong, she set it free, but before it left, it stopped on the window ledge, turned, and to her great surprise sang. (*Sings*.) "They'll be bluebirds over, the white cliffs of Dover, tomorrow ..." See there she goes.

(*THEY both watch, as though they see it fly away. RAY taps LV, and smiles*.)

RAY. Eh, true that. (*Gently reaches down and picks up an album from a nearby pile*.) Beautifully taken care of these, the covers and all that. Are you carrying on keeping 'em the same?

LV. He showed me.

RAY. Yeah, wiping 'em before play an' all that?

(SHE nods.)

RAY. Good thing. Collector's items some of them I imagine. Which were his favourites.

LV. Them four there. (*Points to a pile.*)

RAY. Ahh. (*Goes in pocket for paper, gets it out.*) Oh no.

LV. What?

RAY. Well. I was thinking we could a made sure we'd got them in, but we're not doing it now. (*Puts paper back.*)

LV. Oh.

RAY. Bet he would a like that though, your dad, eh? Tribute to his life's love performed by his only daughter. That would a been something wun't it eh? Sounds like he deserved it too. He were a good un eh, your dad?

(LV nods.)

RAY. I bet. Shame. 'Cause let's face it, the man and the music don't get much respect do they, (*Indicates downstairs.*) if you know what I mean.

LV. Ray.

RAY. (*Expectant.*) Yeah?

LV. Nothing.

RAY. (*Thrown, then:*) Look, there she goes again, the bluebird, under the moon and over the stars.

LV. I'll do it.

RAY. (*Casually.*) Oh, okay.

LV. Only once.

RAY. (*Still casual, containing himself.*) Right then. I'm pleased. I'll just nip downstairs for me ciggies, back in a sec. (*HE goes half way downstairs, stops. Faces out. Then, like a bastard. To himself.*) Yes! Yes! Yes!

(*BLACKOUT.*
Suddenly MARI comes bursting out of her room, struggling to do herself up.)

MARI. SADIE! SADIE, come here. Where are you when I need you, frig!

(*MARI carries on down to bottom of stairs, still struggling. SADIE comes out of bathroom and downstairs.*)

MARI. SADIE!

(*SADIE arrives. SHE has a fancy blouse on from 1964 or thereabouts, with ruffled frontage.*)

MARI. Oh thank God for that, I need fastening up. It's harder and harder to get into this stuff, I tell you.

(*SADIE does it for her.*)

MARI. Oh tar, well done Sadie, tar, here have a sherry for your accomplishments. Set you up for tonight as well.
SADIE. Okay.
MARI. Pour me one while you're at it.
SADIE. Okay.

(SADIE pours two. MARI preens and lacquers her hair.)

MARI. Fair old frontage on the blouse there Sade, eh?

(SADIE nods. Sits and sips her sherry.)

MARI. You looking forward to going down tonight then, Sadie? Yes. You stick with me, I'll make sure no one laughs at you. *(MARI lacquers more.)* Ray's worked it all out. He thinks he's taking us all to Tarbyland. I had me doubts about her doing it again but, well he's won me over. I can't say no to him. Oh what a tongue that guy has, half raspberry, half razor. *(Lacquers more.)* And I don't know, maybe for once that fucker fate is smiling down on us. How do you feel, Sade?
SADIE and MARI. Okay.
SADIE. Dokey.
MARI. See, see. *(SHE carries on preening.)* There's certainly some raspberry in the air from somewhere. Oh, sod the devil, I'll put some bit more cheeks on.

(SHE leans into mirror, putting make-up on. RAY comes in silently without her noticing. Puts "ssh" sign up to Sadie. Creeps up behind Mari with a necklace open ready to put round her neck. MARI suddenly sprays lacquer. It goes all in RAY's eyes.)

RAY. Bloody hell. Aarrgh!
MARI. Sorry. Oh my God. I've blinded my God. Oh no!

(RAY shutting and scrunching up his eyes.)

RAY. I'm alright. I'm alright. Here, I got you something. (*Holds out necklace.*)

MARI. Oh, Raymondo, oh, oh. Look here, Sadie. (*Holds it to her neck.*) Fasten it for me, sir.

RAY. Er. (*Hands out, then finding something at sink to wipe his eyes.*) I'm not coming near you.

MARI. I'll do it then. (*SHE does.*) Looky here. Little sparkle neck me. See, Sade. A love token. That's it in' it, Ray?

(*RAY nods.*)

MARI. In some ways, wish I could lash it round me finger. Ha.

(*Holds up engagement finger. RAY drops cloth.*)

RAY. (*To Sadie.*) Well now Sadie, you're looking beautiful tonight, love. Are we gonna get a dance down there tonight then. Eh?

(*SADIE laughing.*)

MARI. (*Quickly in.*) Sadie, go upstairs now, see if she's ready, the star.

(*SADIE does.*)

RAY. Can't wait Mari, can you? I'm buzzing fit to bust. Are you?

MARI. (*Unsure.*) Yeah.

RAY. What's up wi' you?

MARI. Oh X-Ray, you can see right through me, can't you? It's just, what the sod hell are we to expect tonight?

RAY. Mari. Mari, dove. Don't you worry 'bout a thing. All you have to do is be your radiant self as always.

MARI. Aay, Dr. Ray, you can make me better with just a look and a word.

(SHE goes to kiss him but as SHE does, LV appears at top of stairs. RAY moves away from Mari. LV is wearing a long, to the ground, incredible, figure-hugging, glittering show business dress.)

RAY. Aye, yes, hey, here she comes!

(SADIE brings LV down. LV is blank faced and looking "not there.")

MARI. Aye, here she is.

RAY. Let me open that door. The door that leads to success.

(RAY gets door. SADIE slips a comically inappropriate brightly coloured little plastic mac on LV's shoulders.)

MARI. Hey, get Sadie, the minder. (SHE does a karate chop.)

(THEY set to leave in a procession almost. LV looking down, SADIE behind her, RAY and then MARI.)

MARI. And looky here, LV. (*Prinks necklace.*) Prink, prink. (*As THEY leave.*) As we leave, star spangling down the club, the artiste, the minder, the manager and the Mum.

(*Door BANGS behind them. LIGHTS of the house flicker, flicker but remain on.*
BLACKOUT.
The club. MR. BOO at the mike.)

MR. BOO. Testing, testing. Mr. Boo here. Don't say my name too loud you'll give me a fright. No, now then. Ladies and gentlemen, forgive me if I get serious for a moment, what do you mean I never got funny? No, we've a return act for tonight, "Little Voice." I think you'll agree that last time the voice was there but the rest was little. Now I know we're a tough club, a hard club, and proud of it. And acts fall like flies in here. But I put in a plea if I dare for this girl. I put in a request if I may, for a bit of order, a little support if you could, people, for the girl with the greats queueing in her gullet, shy little, Little Voice, ladies and gentlemen. Little Voice Hoff from down our way.

(*RAY brings on a blindfolded LV and leads her to the center of the stage. HE turns her upstage, back to the audience, removes the blindfold and signals for the music to begin. Exits.*
ORCHESTRATION begins. LV slowly turns around. Sings abbreviated versions of a selection of her best impersonations.
MUSIC ends.
LV in arms up, Garland pose.)

BLACKOUT.
LIGHT UP.
THEY all burst in. MARI first, then RAY, then BOO, LV
  and SADIE. THEY have loads of booze with them.)

RAY. What about that, then?

(Starts opening drinks. SADIE gets LV to the settee and
  sits her down.)

MR. BOO. Marvellous. Oh my God. Tears down
cheeks.

(MARI screaming out.)

RAY. See 'em all standing up. *(Imitates applause.)*

(MARI screaming out.)

RAY. Here we go. *(Popping a shaken beer can,*
spraying everywhere.) Ale and everything all round.

(THEY all get into the drinks, except LV alone on settee,
  staring out.)

MR. BOO. Well, Ray, I can safely say your bookin's
assured down there. And have you, have you ever thought
of the Monaco Club?
RAY. Well, yes. Bloody, yes. Hey, Mari, we might be
doing the Monaco Club an' all.

*(MARI screaming. SHE puts on "their song." Starts jiving
with SADIE., who just remains standing still, with one
arms out, while MARI holds on to her hand and does it.
SADIE looks ill.)*

RAY. *(To Mr. Boo.)* Oh yes, Monaco for a bit, Mr.
Boo, I'll not say no, at this stage who would? But you
know as well as me that soon not even the Monaco is
going to be big enough for this.

*(LV, exhausted, hears, starts shaking her head. No one can
see.)*

RAY. Mr. Boo ...
MR. BOO. Do call me Lou.
RAY. Mr. Boo ...
MR. BOO. Lou.
RAY. Lou, let me tell you. This is the greatest act
going, this. We'll be in London before Christmas, or the
cruises or the telly. Take it, take it from me.
LV. *(Shaking her head.)* Once ...
MR. BOO. I hear what you're saying there, Ray. But I
hope you'll not forget where you got your start.
LV. Once was said.
MR. BOO. What was that, LV? What's she on about? I
can't hear her.
RAY. *(Popping another bottle.)* Is Sadie alright?

*(MR. BOO looks too. SADIE looks a bit ill, vacant,
staring out. MARI stops dancing on Sadie's arm, and
looks at her. Then to Ray.)*

MARI. Sadie, Sadie May! She's alright. She's alright, aren't you?

(SHE slaps Sadie on the back, SADIE hiccups at this. MARI goes towards bottle RAY is holding, THEY all turn away to pour. SADIE has a little dribbly sick down her blouse. But just remains standing where she is.)

RAY. We on for the whole week then, Lou?
MR. BOO. It's yours, Ray.

(LV passes out.)

MR. BOO. I've cancelled the Silverados and Gringo Hodges to have it free for you. I couldn't do nothing else, they were going mad in there.
RAY. I know.
MR. BOO. Wouldn't leave me alone.
RAY. I know. I saw.
MR. BOO. "When?" "When's she on again?" and all that.
RAY. *(Drinks.)* Yes. Yessss!
Mr. BOO. *(To Mari.)* You must be proud, Mrs. Hoff.

(MARI screams.)

RAY. By the way, Sadie's been sick.
MARI. Oh, bloody hell, *(To Sadie.)* Sadie! Sink and wipe. Sink and wipe.

(SADIE moves off on her own in direction of sink. MARI pours herself another.)

MR. BOO. Well, Ray. (*Lifting glass.*) To the rise of Little Voice.

RAY. (*Raising his glass.*) Up tut' sky. Up tut' sky.

(*MARI turns just in time to lift her glass to join the others.*)

RAY. Cheers!

MR. BOO. Cheers!

(*PHONE rings. MARI picks phone up. Screams down it. Puts it back down. Turns to see LV has passed out on settee. Looks again.*)

MARI. What's this. RAY! RAY!

(*RAY comes over.*)

MARI. Oh God, has the little bird bleated and died wi' all the shock!

RAY. She's alright. Just the excitement, that's all.

MR. BOO. Loosen her clothes.

(*RAY starts to loosen LV's clothes. MR. BOO turns off MUSIC.*)

MARI. (*Stopping him.*) I'll do that.

(*SHE tries but is fumbling, too drunk. SADIE comes through, lifts LV and starts to carry her slowly upstairs.*)

MARI. (*Taken aback.*) Oh, aye, tar, Sadie.

(*SADIE goes slowly upstairs. RAY, MARI and MR BOO watching in silence, not moving, for as long as it takes for SADIE to carry her to her room.*)

MR. BOO. "Blessed are the meek for they shall inherit the earth." When, eh, when?
RAY. Eh?

(*MARI turns the record player back up. The LIGHTS blow.*
BLACKOUT.
Some days later. Evening. Alley lit by lamp only. BILLY is crouching there with a lamp, shining it on and off through her window. No response.)

BILLY. LV. (*Flashes light.*) LV. (*Flashes light.*) You're there. (*Flashes light.*) I know you're there. (*Flashes light.*) Can't you see me light? I've come every night since we last spoke. (*Flashes light.*) I'm worried. I know that they're making you do it again and again and again. Are you alright? (*Flashes light. Flashes light, almost like a morse code. No response.*) The lights, LV, I've gone ahead and started setting up. Getting stuff down. So much is needed. (*Flashes light.*) LV. I feel you flickering, fading away. I don't know how, it's like when one of my lights is ready to go, I feel it, I just know. (*Flashes light, really fast one after another. No response. Starts to flash slow, slow again.*) I know if I can get you to the lights they'll lift you. I know they will because I'm doing it for you. I've not said that to you yet, but I'm doing them for you. (*Flashes light.*) LV. (*Flashes light.*) LV. LV. I'll not leave you. I'll be back.

(*HE gives up, turns LIGHT slowly down, as lights come slowly up on next scene.*
LIGHTS UP on living room.[same evening as the last scene] the evening of a performance. LV is in her room in bed. All around her unopened presents. Bouquets of flowers beginning to fade. Downstairs, MARI sits on settee, looking out, drinking. SADIE is slowly making sandwiches on the kitchen table. Silence, except for the soft sound of sandwiches being made. MARI drinks. SADIE works. SADIE finishes, puts last sandwich on plate, and begins to set off upstairs with them. As SHE passes Mari.)

MARI. Here, give us them, Sadie. I'll take 'em up. (*MARI takes tray and goes upstairs. Goes in LV's room.*) LV, love.

(*LV doesn't respond.*)

MARI. Come on, you can't stay there all day and night. I've brought you something to eat, you've got to eat, you've not ate now for four days. What about I put some music on then, some of your music, see what you think, eh?

(*LV gives no response. MARI lifts the sandwiches above her head like she's going to throw them down.*)

MARI. I'm ready to throw these butties all over you. I will, you know I will. (*SHE stares down, no movement. SHE sadly puts them on table by her and leaves. Goes downstairs.*) She won't touch 'em, Sadie. She's not touched anything else we've left either, cup of stone cold tea there. She's on soon. She'll have to bloody go. I wonder if we're pushing her too hard, you know. Four, five spots at the club already. One show after another. She'll not die, Sadie will she? Die off? She's only frail, you know, like her father was before her. Have a to ring Doctor Sock? I don't know. I'll wait for Ray, he'll be here in a minute. I don't know what to do any more. Come and sit by me, Sadie.

(*SADIE does.*)

MARI. Look at me. Am I a good mother, am I doing right? I mean, she's making money now, I mean it's setting her off on something. In the long run, she'll thank me for it, won't she? There's always suffering and struggle in't there, and then they make it in the end. I've cheered up now. Tar for t'advice, Sadie. Don't know what I'd do without you. (*Half to herself.*) You patient fat get.

(*The PHONE rings.*
SHE picks it up. SADIE heads for stairs. MARI covers mouthpiece.)

MARI. Are you going up for a go?

(*SADIE nods. MARI nods. MARI speaks into phone. SADIE goes upstairs.*)

MARI. Hello. Oh is that the local rag? (*Goes posh.*) No, no, she's not available for interviews, best try tomorrow, thanking you. (*Puts phone down.*) Now then.

(*Door opens. RAY comes in. Looking more affluent. HE is smoking a cigar.*)

MARI. Darling. (*SHE throws her arms around him.*)
RAY. Alright Mari, alright. Where is she?
MARI. Ray?
RAY. Yeah.
MARI. Er, don't know how to ...
RAY. What?
MARI. Can she not have this night off?
RAY. Not tonight, no. I've got Bunny Morris coming to see her, this could be a proper break. This could even mean telly.
MARI. Telly?
RAY. Telly.
MARI. Telly?
RAY. Telly.

(*RAY plugs kettle in, it FLASHES.*)

RAY. You wanna watch that! Bugger me. (*HE rinses out a cup, has a drink of water.*)
MARI. Ray ...
RAY. Yeah.
MARI. Er, don't know how to ...
RAY. What?

MARI. Any money sorted yet? I've only had a five and your dead mam's necklace.

RAY. Mari, I keep saying, leave it with me, it's all being carefully proportioned. Me and Boo is in fact just finalising a new contract. I'll let you read it when it's done.

MARI. Oh no, no, no need for that. Just lob the doubloons into me open handbag when they's ready.

RAY. Right then. You picked up them dresses from the dry cleaners, din't you?

MARI. Oh.

RAY. Don't tell me what I think you're going to tell me, please don't.

(MARI opening and closing her mouth like a fish, not knowing what to do.)

RAY. Don't.

(MARI continues fish.)

RAY. You forgot, din't you?

(MARI nods.)

RAY. Oh no!

MARI. I've been so busied, Ray.

RAY. Bloody hell. (*HE boots the pouffe.*)

MARI. Hey, watch me furniture!

RAY. She's on any minute.

MARI. I know! I know! Oh so sorry, darling. (*Goes to embrace him.*) Don't be crossy wid your rolling puss puss.

RAY. Never mind all that, she'll have to wear one of
her old ones.

MARI. Yes. Yes she must.

RAY. What's she got?

MARI. What's she got? What's she got? I don't know.

RAY. Ooh!

MARI. SADIE! (*Suddenly remembers.*) Wait a minute,
I think there's one in the dirty wash.

RAY. Bloody hell!

MARI. It's alright, I'll iron it.

*(SHE gets dress out. Tries putting the ironing board up and
nearly kills herself. SADIE has arrived by this time.
SHE and RAY watch in amazement.)*

MARI. Save me, Sadie! Save me.

SADIE. Okay.

(SADIE takes over the ironing. MARI goes to Ray.)

MARI. Ray Milland, you still my friend, ain't you?
Eh? Eh?

RAY. We can't have this, Mari. I'm going to have to
get someone else to look after her.

MARI. What you on about, I'm her mother.

RAY. Are you?

MARI. Yes. And you're my man.

RAY. Am I?

MARI. Ray, Ray, what you saying?

*(HE walks away. SHE turns, kicks something flying, then
turns to Sadie.)*

MARI. You're too quiet to be my friend, you. Fuck off.

(SADIE goes. Silence until SHE leaves, then MARI picks iron up and starts ironing. SHE is slipping all over the place.)

MARI. I'm doing it now, Ray love. Yes I am. I'll flatten it just so, once I've got me legs right.
RAY. Leave it, you're gonna get burnt in a minute.

(MARI carries on frantically ironing, trying.)

RAY. LEAVE IT!

(SHE stops. Pause. HE goes and gets dress.)

RAY. It'll have to do.

(HE is about to walk away, SHE grabs his hand.)

MARI. *(Pleading.)* Ray.
RAY. Leave it, Mari.
MARI. You're always rushing away, Ray.
RAY. There's a lot to do.
MARI. Ray, kiss me. *(SHE strains towards him.)*
RAY. Oh, get off.
MARI. Ray?
RAY. *(Getting away.)* Stop clinging on me!
MARI. *(Coming close again.)* Don't spoil it, Ray! We go together so well.

RAY. Go together well! Go to ... Don't kid yourself woman, we go nowhere. For a start, you're past it, your body's gone. When your clothes go, I can't keep track of it, it's all over the place. Too many maulings, Mari. And you're too loud and you stink of drink. That's alright for where you belong, the alley wall, the back of a car, flat on your back on a rug. But no way could you come with me and her to better things. No way love. Look at yourself, look, lumping out your crazy clothes, just about keeping your balance. Christ, do you think I don't have birds I go to, do you not think it's like putting my face in flowers after you. You've had it Mari, you're nowt now but something for after the boozer, a chaser, a takeaway, a bit of a laugh. All you've ever had that I want sits up there. And all you're doing is getting in the way, woman. You were in the way the night I heard her, that night I heard her singing, and you're still in the way now. For Godsake wise up and fuck off.

(HE grabs up the dress and rushes upstairs. MARI is shattered, arms out in front, like a drunk lost thing, broken. Reaching out, SHE walks out the door almost in a trance.)

MARI. Sadie. Sadie. Sadie.

(RAY has arrived upstairs. LV is still in the bed.)

RAY. Here, get this on, we're late. Come on. Come on. I've had enough of you lot tonight.

(LV doesn't respond.)

RAY. Dress on.

(SHE doesn't respond.)

RAY. Get this on.

(HE grabs her up. SHE's limp in his hand. HE slaps her. At that, voices begin to rush out of her uncontrollably, some sung, some spoken.
Judy Garland (JG), Piaf (P), Marilyn Monroe (MM), Shirley Bassey (SB), Billy Holiday (BH), Cilla Black (CB), Gracie Fields (GF)

LV. (BH) "Stop haunting me now, just leave me alone." (SB) "This is my life."
RAY. Hey.
LV. (JG) Toto, toto.
RAY. Stop it.
LV. (SB) "Let me live. Oh let me live."
RAY. Stop it, I'm warning you!
LV. (MM) "Look what you started. A conflagration, baby, that's what." (SB) "But if you go I won't cry."
RAY. Stop this.
LV. (BH) "You go your way and I go mine, it's best that we do."
RAY. Save it for tonight.
LV. (SB) "I, I who have nothing, I, I who have no one." (MM) "But my heart belongs to Daddy."
RAY. Damn you LV. *(RAY is backing off a bit now with the sheer force of it.)*

LV. (CB) "Something tells me, something's gonna happen tonight."

RAY. Oh no.

LV. (JG) "If you let me, let me, let me." (SB) "With my nose pressed up against the window pane."

RAY. Not mad. Not now please.

LV. (P) "... Da Da Da Da Da Da ..."

RAY. Don't crack now, LV. NOO!

LV. (P) "... Da Da Da Da Da Da ..." Encore, milord.

RAY. No.

LV. (MM) "I'm tired of getting the fuzzy end of the lollipop."

RAY. Please, LV.

LV. (JG) "You go away or I'll bite you myself." (SB) "This is me. This is me."

RAY. Is it too late? Come back!

LV. (JG) "I guess when you met me it was just one of those things."

RAY. Oh my God. Come wi' me. (*RAY beckons to her.*)

LV. (SB) "Beckons you to enter his web of sin, but don't go in." (*P, in French.*) "For at last I happen to be strong."

(*RAY is knocked back onto his knees.*)

RAY. I pray you, LV. We was on our way together.

LV. (JG) "Happy together, unhappy together." (MM) "See what I mean, not very bright." (JG) "I'm going to haunt you so, I'm going to taunt you so, I'm going to drive you to ruin."

(Spins around and knocks RAY who falls downstairs. HE holds his mouth.)

RAY. Me teeth.
LV. (GF) "Never mind your teeth, leave 'em out."

(RAY is at bottom of stairs. HE looks up, SHE is still going from voice to voice, oblivious.)

LV. (JG) "Zing, zing, zing." *(SHE goes back in her room.)* (CB) "Step inside love, and stay, step inside love, step inside love." (SB) "Just an empty room, full of empty space, like the empty look I see on your face." (GF) "Sally, Sally, pride of our alley."

(RAY, devastated, rushes out, SLAMS the door. With the force of the slam, the iron falls off the ironing board. SOCKET EXPLODES. LIGHTS CRACK and a FLAME rips around the ceiling and wall sides. A FIRE begins. LV in her room, still going from one voice to another.)

LV. (JG) "Run Toto, run Toto. He got away. He got away." (P) "Bravo, bravo."

(The sound of FIRE below, SMOKE is rising and into the room. SHE is oblivious to it. Smoke almost covering her.)

LV. (JG) "'Cos when you're crying, don't you know that your make-up starts to run, and your eyes get red and scrappy." (P) "Both the good and the bad I have flung in the fire." (MM) "But, baby, I like it hot." (JG) "Glory, glory, hallelujah, glory, glory, hallelujah, his truth is marching on." (JG) "There's no place like home. There's no place like home. There's no place like home. There's no place like home. "

(Suddenly the "Cherry Picker" appears high in the alley and glides up to the window. BILLY is in it. HE breaks the window with his hammer, opens it and gets her out. Still she is going from voice to voice as the machine takes them away and down the alley.)
BLACKOUT.

(The club is packed. MR. BOO excited and worried. His toupee on tilt. Sweat pouring off him. Caught in mid-speech...)

MR. BOO. Calm down. Calm down. Sorry she's late. She'll be here any minute. I assure you. Look, sit down at the back! I never thought we could get so many in. What a star turn eh! Calm down. She'll be here soon! *(To someone.)* Look stop that! *(To someone.)* Put that back woman!

(Suddenly, the opening strains of the song 'It's Over', Roy Orbison, come on from the juke box.)

MR. BOO. Hey get that bloody juke box off! Who's put that on.

(RAY comes toward stage. BOO sees him.)

MR. BOO. Ray Say's here.

(RAY comes straight on, grabs the mike without looking at BOO and walks to center stage, BOO following him.)

MR. BOO. Where is she Ray? Where is she?

(RAY pushes MR. BOO away.)

MR. BOO. Hey, who you shoving. *(Sees something's up.)* What you playing at, give me that. *(Reaches for mike.)* Here.

(RAY suddenly threatens him, very violently, with mike held low like a broken bottle. BOO backs off. BOO signals off-stage to someone. Then goes off himself. RAY turns to audience, dishevelled, some blood on his mouth and nose, sings to some of the lyrics, talks over others.)

RAY. *(Sings out.)* 'Golden days before they end.' *(Looking out into audience, hand shielding light.)* Bunny Morris. Bunny TV Morris. Where are you? Wherever you are. The bastard drinks are on me.

(Sings.) 'Your baby won't be near you any more.' Not tonight, not any night! *(Sings out.)* 'Tender nights before they fly! Aye mine has. *(Sings.)* 'falling stars that seem to cry.' Aye true that's what they do. Can't hack it.

Ladies and gentlemen, I had a dream. *(Flicks mike lead. Sings.)* 'It's over.'

When I think what might have been. *(Spits.)*

(Sings.) 'It breaks my heart in two.'

Finished.

(Sings.) 'We're through.'

All through, THROUGH.

(Sings.) 'It's over. It's over.'

(Suddenly juke box is turned off, record cuts out, he carries on.)

(Sings.) 'Over, over, OVER!!'

(Stops, puts mike back in stand. Leans head on it. Long long pause. Silence. Slowly he lifts his head. Slowly he walks off. BOO has reappeared, we watch RAY go.)

(BLACKNESS. The same night. Later.)

(The living room is burnt out, charred furniture and soot everywhere, things melted and scorched. MARI and SADIE come in silhouetted in door. It's too dark for them to see. MARI tries light switch. Nothing.)

SADIE. I'll get me torch.

(SADIE goes. MARI strikes a match and sees everything. She gasps. The match goes out. She's still very shaken and slaughtered. SADIE comes back with a torch. Turns it on.)

MARI. Look at the bloody crap of it. Me last home and testament gone up in flames, burnt to buggery. Sadie, I'm gutted. I'm gutted tut' twat bone wi' all this. Look at me ornaments, look at me home. Sadie, Sadie try getting some sugar now, it'll be caramel burnt. I tell you. You might like it, but I wouldn't. I wouldn't.

(The phone rings.)

MARI. I told you about this phone din't I? Din't I? I knew it had some science to it. *(She picks up melted phone.)* Hello, hell here. *(Listens.)* You got wrong number.

(MARI puts phone down.)

SADIE. Who were that?
MARI. Some official bastard wanting to know if Mari Hoff was still alive. Now then. Oh, Sadie, when I need picking up off the ceiling and the floor, who's left, but you, hey Sade? Hey, who thinks about me, but you. You're a friend, all lard and love, ain't you? Come here. *(Hugs her.)* Sadie, your armpits have that smell of cat food again, what have I told you? Wash there.
SADIE. Okay.
MARI. Okay, rub-a-dub. Bloody hell, at least I'll be able to find you in the dark. Oh, what am I to do, Sade. Let's look up, might not be as bad.

(THEY go upstairs. MARI goes in her bedroom. Screams a little. Comes out.)

MARI. All gone. Hopeless. Barbecued bed. Doorless wardrobes full of cinders. *(SHE opens the door to LV's room.)* Well, look at this, would you believe it? Only singed. *(Sees records.)* Look, look what's not burnt. Look, the seeds of my downfall, the bitter beanstalk beaning circle beginnings that broke Mother's back. They go now. *(SHE lets them fall out of their covers through the open window. THEY tumble into the alley and smash.)* Oh yes, they go now. *(SHE stands next to the bed punching the faces on the LP covers.)* You and you and you.

You took my husband, played his heart till it stopped. You took my daughter, my walls. Take that. *(SHE throws them out too, all out of their covers so they smash below.)* There, there. Down you go into smithereen alley. Crescendo. Crescendo on that hard gutter floor. I'm coming too.

(SHE climbs onto window sill. SADIE grabs her back. Holds her waist. SHE flops forward like a rag doll in SADIE's arms. Suddenly THEY hear a van pulling up. THEY look out the window.)

MARI. *(To SADIE.)* Out with the light. Hide.

(THEY are heard scuttling about in the dark. Then stillness as the door opens and BILLY and LV come in. THEY stand silhouetted in the doorway.)

BILLY. I don't think you should be here. It's too dark. Come on away.

(LV just stands.)

BILLY. I'm not sure you should be.

(LV just stands.)

BILLY. Come on, let's go. You can get whatever you want tomorrow in the light. Come on, Little Voice.

(BILLY turns to go, taking her with him. SHE stops him pleadingly.)

LV. *(Almost inaudible.)* Please.

BILLY. I've some lights from work in the van, let me fetch them in.

(HE goes out. LV stays in the dark. BILLY comes in with the lights. When HE puts them down they illuminate the room, one orange, one yellow. They are the self-contained light units used around holes, etc. They make the place look like a set for hell in an old theatre melodrama. Their faces are illuminated strangely from below in the orange and yellow lights and massive shadows are thrown up the back.)

BILLY. Shall I stay with you?

LV. No.

BILLY. I'll wait outside.

LV. No.

BILLY. You can't stay here on your... Okay, I'll nip back down the club. I'll finish off, then come back for you. Wait by the corner. Don't stay in here.

(LV doesn't answer. HE looks at her. HE kisses her gently on the face. HE goes.

LV turns to stairs and makes her way up. Suddenly, bedroom door bursts open and MARI comes out.)

MARI. What happened, eh? What happened here, then!

LV. *(Screams.)* Aarrgh!

(MARI pursues her. LV backs downstairs.)

MARI. The little match girl who goes burning everything,

everything, everything down then.

(LV frantically shakes her head.)

    MARI. Yes. Yes. My house is a stub. My home a grate.

(LV is at the foot of the stairs.)

    MARI. Now then girl.

(MARI goes to grab her. Suddenly SADIE sits up from floor between them, LV screams again.)

    MARI. Sadie!
    SADIE. Sorry.

(SADIE gets up and goes out.)

    MARI. *(To LV.)* Where's your burns?

(LV looks scared.)

    MARI. Exactly. They is none.

(MARI charges at her. LV runs. MARI falls on settee. Mounds of soot fly up into the air. SHE slowly sits up on the settee facing out. SHE grabs up the phone and throws it up back. The orange and yellow lights strangely illuminating her face from below, her shadow thrown huge at the back.)

    MARI. I'm now in the carcass of my house, a smoked ham.

I can't start again. What's the next move. I'm too beat for a man, really I ask you. I've been jumping the coals for years, now I've finally fallen in. Nobody wants the burnt bits, have you noticed. They love a blazing bint but when the flames have gone who wants the char? Well, some might say I've got what I deserve. But that's the problem, I've never had what I deserved. I was more than this dump I had to live in. IN fact, my energy itself could have burnt this place down years ago, four times over with fireworks forever. I was more than what I married. Your father, your father kissing me with his parlor lips. I had health and breasts and legs. I strode. When I got behind your pram I propelled it about a hundred miles an hour. The air was full of the sound of wolf whistles, deafening. He was shambling somewhere behind, a beanpole Chaplain. But you, you were always his. It was always you and him, you and him all the time, doing quiet things, heads bent together, listening to the records. Driving me mad, my energy could have burnt this house down four times over and you two tilted into books, listening to the radio shows, playing board games in front of the fire. Fuck it. And now I'm dancing on my own grave and it's a roasting tin. My house gutted, my last possession gone. My last chance charred. Look at me up to my ankles in char. *(Looking at all the thick soot over the floor.)* In fact, this is my soul leaking over the floor here, soot itself. I'm going to scoop handfuls up and spread it over you. Your head, you see, was the match head to this. *(Indicating everything.)*

(SHE gets up with her hands full of soot, and traps LV in a corner. Holding her with one hand while SHE prepares to cover her with the soot from the other, SHE holds her there, then:)

MARI. Wait a minute. No. What do you want anyway? Oh, I know, your records. *(SHE lets her go.)* The firemen put all the salvage in the alley. They should be there.

(LV goes out and round to the alley. MARI stays put. LV sees the big pile of broken records almost filling the alley. Lamplight glinting off them. SHE gently picks a piece up. Opens her mouth to scream but nothing comes out. Opens her mouth again, nothing. MARI appears.)

MARI. What's up, cat got your tongue?

(MARI steps forward but SHE slips on the massive pile of broken records, slithering all over in them and falls. LV quickly holds the sharp edge of a half record to her throat. MARI suddenly stunned.)

LV. And now, you will listen! One time, one! *(LV screams.)* There's one. *(Screams again.)* There's another. Can you hear me now my mother! *(Words rush out.)* My dad, you mention him and it's wrong what you say, wrong what you say. You drove him as fast as you could to an early grave. With your men and your shouting and your pals and your nights, your nights, your nights, your nights, your nights of neglect. Things forgotten everywhere. No soap in the dish, no roll in the toilet, no clean blouse for school. Oh my dad, when he had his records on he sparkled, not dazzling like you, but with fine lights, fine lights! He couldn't speak up to you, 'cause he must have wanted you so. I couldn't speak up to you, 'cause I could never get a word in! *(Looks at piece of record in her hand.)* These become my tongues. *(Drops it.)* And now they've gone, I don't know where this is coming from. But it's one after another and I can tell you now. *(Pause.)* That you hurt me. *(Pause.)* With your sharp ways and the things you said and your SELFISHNESS WOMAN! *(Pause.)* I've got to stop now. I'm trembling so strange.

(SHE drifts slowly away. MARI on her knees, trying to stand. Pleading.)

MARI. LV, I beseech you. I beseech you, LV. *(MARI is slipping, trying to stand but slipping in all the records. Soot all over her hands and face, in the lamplight, slipping, sliding, trying to stand.)* I beseech you! I beseech you!

(SHE stops struggling flops face down in the pile.
SHE closes her eyes. SADIE is at alley end, peeping and softly giggling.
BLACKOUT.
LIGHTS come up on the empty club. LV comes in, stands at back of stage. Suddenly, faint purring sound of machinery. LV looks up. BILLY comes into view in "Cherry Picker.")

BILLY. You come back on your own. I was just coming. Everything alright?

(SHE nods.)

BILLY. I've just to fit this last un, then it's done.

(SHE nods. HE has installed his own expensive and amazing lights and effects into the club rig and all around. HE

operates them from a hand-held remote control.)

BILLY. Right. First a few lights.

(HE presses control, LIGHTS come on beautifully, spraying colors, then soaking the stage in deep blue.)

BILLY. And music.

(HE presses control. Powerful orchestral arrangement of a song comes on. HE changes lights again, again, through the building introduction, and incredible display. SHE is awestruck at it all, dizzied by it.)

BILLY. You might recognize this one. Sing if you feel like it.

(SHE looks at him.)

BILLY. Sing, Little Voice. Go on.

(The LIGHTS suddenly become so powerful that they seem to lift her in the air, the music too. SHE closes her eyes, starts to sing, quiet at first, SHE opens her eyes to see millions of tiny white lights sprayed all over the stage. SHE sings louder holding up her hands like catching snow or stars.)

BILLY. Go on, louder.

(HE changes the lights again. SHE sings out.)

BILLY. Sing for yourself.

(SHE sings out, stepping forward, louder, clearer as the LIGHTS beat and flash higher and higher weaving breathtaking patterns.)

BILLY. You're singing in your own voice. Your own.

(SHE's singing full, confident, loud, tears coming down her face. SHE moves as SHE sings now. SHE's near the "Cherry Picker.")

BILLY. Get in. Go on. Go on.

(SHE does. BILLY operates the "Picker" it begins to ascend as SHE sings. Sings. The "Picker" rising higher and higher. HE changes to lasers, beautiful beams, breathtaking patterns across the space. SHE rises into them higher and higher, up in the lights, singing, singing, singing in her own voice.)

THE END

About the Author

Jim Cartwright lives in Lancashire, where he was born.

Road, his first play, opened at the royal Court Theatre in 1986, was revived again at the Royal Court that same year, and again in 1987, before being taken on a nationwide tour. It won the Samuel Beckett Award, *Drama* magazine's Best New Play Award and was joint winner of the George Devine Award and the Plays and Players' Best New Play Award.

His other work for theatre includes *Bed* at the Royal National Theatre in 1989; *Two* at the Bolton Octagon Theatre in 1989, transferring to the Young Vic, London in 1990, (winner of the *Manchester Evening News* Best New Play Award); *The Rise and Fall of Little Voice* at the Royal National Theatre in 1992, and at the Aldwych Theatre later that year (winner of the *Evening Standard* Award for Best comedy in 1992 and the Olivier Award for Best Comedy in 1993). He wrote and directed *I Licked a Slag's Deodorant*, for the Royal Court Theatre Upstairs at the Ambassadors Theatre in 1996.

Other works include, for radio: *Baths*, BBC in 1987; for television: *Road*, BBC in 1987 (winner of the Golden Nymph Award for Best Film); *Vroom*, Channel Four 1988 (Selected as Centerpiece at the London Film Festival); *June*, BBC 1990; *Wedded*, BBC 1990, *Bed*, BBC 1994.

Also By
Jim Cartwright

Road

Two

Please visit our website **samuelfrench.com** for complete
descriptions and licensing information

OTHER TITLES AVAILABLE FROM SAMUEL FRENCH

ROAD
Jim Cartwright

Dramatic Comedy / 8m, 6f or 4m, 3f / Unit Set
During one wild night, a drunken guide conducts a tour of Road,
his derelict Lancashire street, where sharp and comic scenes jos-
tle viciously to expose a population driven mad by despair.

"Uncomfortable and magical ... funny and bitter. It is a
northern *Under Milk Wood*, high on pills and booze."
– The London Sunday Times

"The climax comes when two flash lads have picked up two
girls.... This sequence is simply one of the most unlikely,
audacious and, in the event, riveting scenes to be found cur-
rently in the theatre."
– London Financial Times

"Beneath the gags, the playwright's rumbling sense of lost
dignity resulting from unemployment, chauvinism or from
simply getting paralytically pissed, give this stunning debut a
perceptive and frightening reality."
– City Limits

"Mr. Cartwright is asking the right question and he has
something to say. The question is, why is the world so hard?"
– London Observer

"The debut of a writer of outstanding talent."
– London Sunday Telegraph

OTHER TITLES AVAILABLE FROM SAMUEL FRENCH

TWO
Jim Cartwright

Comic Drama / 1m, 1f / Interior

A bickering husband and wife and the dozen regulars who pass through their pub in an evening are played by two actors. Each vignette skillfully combines pathos and humor. When a little boy is left behind by his father, a fragile reconciliation occurs as their own dark tragedy is revealed

"Astonishing, funny and sad."
– *Daily Express*

"Entertainment of a very high caliber."
– *Sunday Correspondent*

"Vastly entertaining."
– *Jewish Chronicle*

"Go to laugh and be moved."
– *City Limits*

"Absolutely riveting."
– *Daily Telegraph*